A+ Alphabet Books

A Rain Forest ABC

An Alphabet Book

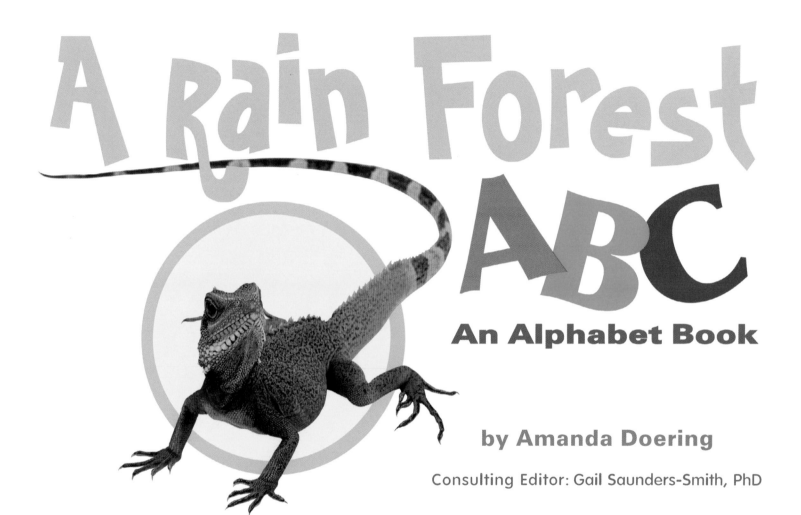

by Amanda Doering

Consulting Editor: Gail Saunders-Smith, PhD

Capstone press

Mankato, Minnesota

A is for ant.

Ants are tiny creatures that carry big loads. They cut leaves and carry them back to their nest.

B is for butterfly.

Beautiful butterflies flutter by. Butterflies come in all colors, from bright yellow to brilliant blue.

C is for camouflage.

Some insects use camouflage to hide
in the forest. This bug looks just like a leaf.

D is for dung beetle.

Do you know what dung is? It's animal doo.
Dung beetles dine on dung for dinner.

5

E is for eyelash viper.

An eyelash viper sees a meal creeping by.
If this snake winks at you, don't stop
to say, "hi."

F is for fern.

Ferns blanket the rain forest floor. Their leaves are home to insects, frogs, lizards, and more.

G is for gorilla.

Gorillas aren't fierce giants. They are actually quite shy. Gorillas pad through forests, keeping out of sight.

H is for hummingbird.

Is it a bug or a bird? It's a hummingbird. These tiny birds hover in the air, sipping nectar from rain forest flowers.

9

I is for iguana.

Iguanas wanna climb trees to look for food. They crawl along finding fruit and leaves.

J is for jaguar.

Can you spot the jaguar? This cat's spotted coat helps it hide in the forest.

K is for katydid.

Katydids sing in rain forest trees. Can you guess where the katydid's ears are? They're on its knees.

L is for lemur.

Lemurs look and listen for danger. Young lemurs learn to stay close to mom.

M is for moss.

Moss grows perfectly in wet places.
It covers trees like a blanket.

N is for nest.

Some birds hang their nests from branches. Hanging nests keep bird eggs safe from snakes.

O is for orangutan.

Orangutans like hanging around. These orange apes spend lots of time off the ground.

16

P is for piranha.

Say, "cheese." A piranha has a nasty smile. This small fish takes big bites with its sharp teeth.

Q is for quetzal.

Can you say quetzal? Say, **"ket-SAHL."**
This shy bird stays out of sight by hiding
in rotting trees.

R is for red-eyed tree frog.

Red-eyed tree frogs leap from tree to tree. Sticky toes help them stick to branches and leaves.

S is for sloth.

Sloths are slowpokes. They creep around trees. Sometimes they move only a few feet a day.

T is for toucan.

Hey, big bill! Toucans have terrific bills.
Their colorful bills attract mates.

U is for uakari monkey.

Is this red-faced monkey embarrassed? No, it's a uakari monkey. You say it, **"wah-KAH-ree."** This monkey's face is red all the time.

V is for vines.

Vines twist and tangle through the trees. Vines weave around the forest like a giant spider web.

W is for waterfall.

Waterfalls wash over rain forest cliffs. Waterfalls are wonderful places for animals to cool off.

X is for extinct.

Every day, about 100 kinds of rain forest plants and animals become extinct. What will rain forests look like if all the plants and animals die? They will be empty like this page.

Y is for Yanomami.

People live in the rain forest too. The Yanomami live off the food they find in the Amazon rain forest.

Z is for zodiac moth.

Zodiac moths rest with their wings spread wide.
The moth has stripes to help it hide.

Fun Facts about Rain Forests

The Amazon rain forest has been called the "Lungs of the Earth." About 20 percent of the world's oxygen is produced by plants in the Amazon rain forest.

As many as 3,000 kinds of fruit grow in the rain forest.

About 1.5 acres (.6 hectare) of rain forest are destroyed every second. Most of the land is logged or cleared for farmland.

More than half the world's plants, animals, and insects live in tropical rain forests.

About 120 kinds of prescription medicines are made from rain forest plants.

Many rain forest animals blend in with their surroundings. Brightly colored parrots look like rain forest flowers. A chameleon's skin becomes lighter or darker to look like leaves. A jaguar's spots look like shadows between plants.

Most tropical rain forests receive 160 to 400 inches (400 to 1,000 centimeters) of rain each year.

Glossary

embarrassed (em-BA-ruhssd)—feeling uncomfortable or awkward; when people are embarrassed, their faces may turn red.

extinct (ek-STINGKT)—to die out; extinct plants and animals no longer exist anywhere in the world.

hover (HUHV-ur)—to remain in one place in the air; hummingbirds hover to drink the nectar from flowers.

insect (IN-sekt)—a small animal with a hard outer shell, six legs, three body sections, and two antennas; most insects have wings.

mate (MATE)—the male or female partner of a pair of animals

nectar (NEK-tur)—a sweet liquid that hummingbirds drink from flowers

Read More

Fowler, Allan. *Living in a Rain Forest.* Rookie Read-About Geography. New York: Children's Press, 2000.

Kratter, Paul. *The Living Rain Forest: An Animal Alphabet.* Watertown, Mass: Charlesbridge, 2004.

Spirin, Ilya. *Rainforest ABC.* New York: Winslow Press, 2000.

Internet Sites

FactHound offers a safe, fun way to find Internet sites related to this book. All of the sites on FactHound have been researched by our staff.

Here's how:
1. Visit *www.facthound.com*
2. Type in this special code **0736826114** for age-appropriate sites. Or enter a search word related to this book for a more general search.
3. Click on the **Fetch It** button.

FactHound will fetch the best sites for you!

Index

A+ Books are published by Capstone Press
151 Good Counsel Drive, P.O. Box 669, Mankato, Minnesota 56002
www.capstonepress.com

1 2 3 4 5 6 09 08 07 06 05 04

Library of Congress Cataloging-in-Publication Data
Doering, Amanda.
   A Rain forest ABC: an alphabet book / by Amanda Doering.
   p. cm.—(A+ alphabet books)
   Includes bibliographical references and index.
   ISBN 0-7368-2611-4 (hardcover)
   1. Rain forest animals—Juvenile literature. 2. Rain forests—Juvenile literature. 3. English language—Alphabet—Juvenile literature. I. Title.
QL112.D59 2005
578.734—dc22   2004000352

Summary: Introduces rain forests through photographs and brief text that uses one word relating to rain forests for each letter of the alphabet.

Credits
Blake A. Hoena and June Preszler, editors; Heather Kindseth, designer; Kelly Garvin, photo researcher; Eric Kudalis, product planning editor

Photo Credits
Ann & Rob Simpson, 15; Artville, LLC, 28 (right); Aurora/Robert Caputo/IPN, 26; Bruce Coleman Inc./Barbara Williams, 7; Bruce Coleman Inc./E.R. Degginger, 23; Bruce Coleman Inc./Gail M. Shumway, 3, 19, 24; Bruce Coleman Inc./George D. Dodge, 2; Bruce Coleman Inc./JC Carton, 20; Bruce Coleman Inc./Joe McDonald, 6, 10; Bruce Coleman Inc./Julie Eggers, 14; Bruce Coleman Inc./Michael Fogden, 9, 18; Corbis/Michael & Patricia Fogden, 4, 5; DigitalVision, 28 (left), 29 (right); DigitalVision/Gerry Ellis & Michael Durham, cover, 27; Erwin and Peggy Bauer, 21; Minden Pictures/Claus Meyer, 17; Minden Pictures/Frans Lanting, 11, 13; Minden Pictures/Gerry Ellis, 8; Minden Pictures/Konrad Wothe, 16; naturepl.com/Pete Oxford, 22; Pete Carmichael, 12; PhotoDisc, 1, 29 (left)

Note to Parents, Teachers, and Librarians
A Rain Forest ABC: An Alphabet Book uses colorful photographs and a nonfiction format to introduce children to characteristics about rain forests while building a mastery of the alphabet. This book is designed to be read independently by an early reader or to be read aloud to a pre-reader. The images help early readers and listeners understand the text and concepts discussed. The book encourages further learning by including the following sections: Fun Facts about Rain Forests, Glossary, Read More, Internet Sites, and Index. Early readers may need assistance using these features.